EARTH
No Place Like Home

by Joyce Markovics

Consultant: Karly M. Pitman, PhD
Planetary Science Institute
Tucson, Arizona

BEARPORT
PUBLISHING

New York, New York

Credits

Cover, © NASA; TOC, © NASA; 4–5, © NASA; 6–7, © Wikipedia & NASA; 8–9, © NASA; 10L, © Iarus/Shutterstock; 10R, © Christopher Wood/Shutterstock; 11L, © Zixian/Shutterstock; 11R, © Betty Shelton/Shutterstock; 12–13, © Willyam Bradberry/Shutterstock; 12B, © CoraMax/Shutterstock; 14–15, © Pal Tervagimov/Shutterstock; 14, © CoraMax/Shutterstock; 16, © Fisherss/Shutterstock; 17, © Mat Hayward/Shutterstock; 18, © Fisherss/Shutterstock; 19, © NASA; 20–21, © Adam Block/NASA/JPL; 23TL, Eniko Balogh/Shutterstock; 23TM, © iStock/Thinkstock; 23TR, © NASA; 23BL, © Wikipedia & NASA; 23BM, © Wikipedia; 23BR, © 113170939; 24, © Fisherss/Shutterstock.

Publisher: Kenn Goin
Senior Editor: Joyce Tavolacci
Creative Director: Spencer Brinker
Design: Debrah Kaiser
Photo Researcher: Michael Win

Library of Congress Cataloging-in-Publication Data

Markovics, Joyce L., author.
    Earth : no place like home / by Joyce Markovics.
        pages cm. — (Out of this world)
    Includes bibliographical references and index.
    ISBN 978-1-62724-563-0 (library binding) — ISBN 1-62724-563-4 (library binding)
    1. Earth (Planet)—Juvenile literature. I. Title.
    QB631.4.M364 2015
    525—dc23
                                        2014037338

For more information, write to Bearport Publishing Company, Inc., 45 West 21st Street, Suite 3B, New York, New York 10010. Printed in the United States of America.

10 9 8 7 6 5 4 3 2 1

CONTENTS

What's the only planet where plants and animals live?

Earth is the third planet from the Sun.

JUPITER

MARS

VENUS

EARTH

MERCURY

SUN

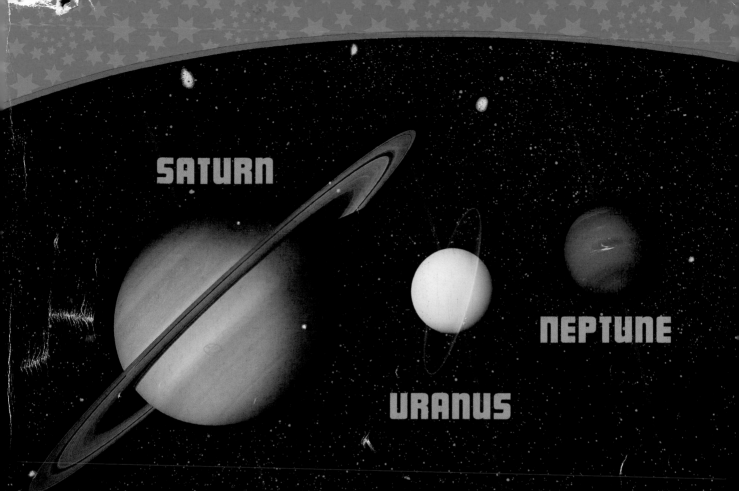

SATURN

URANUS

NEPTUNE

Earth moves around the Sun.

The trip takes 365 days, or one year.

Heat and light from the Sun travel to Earth.

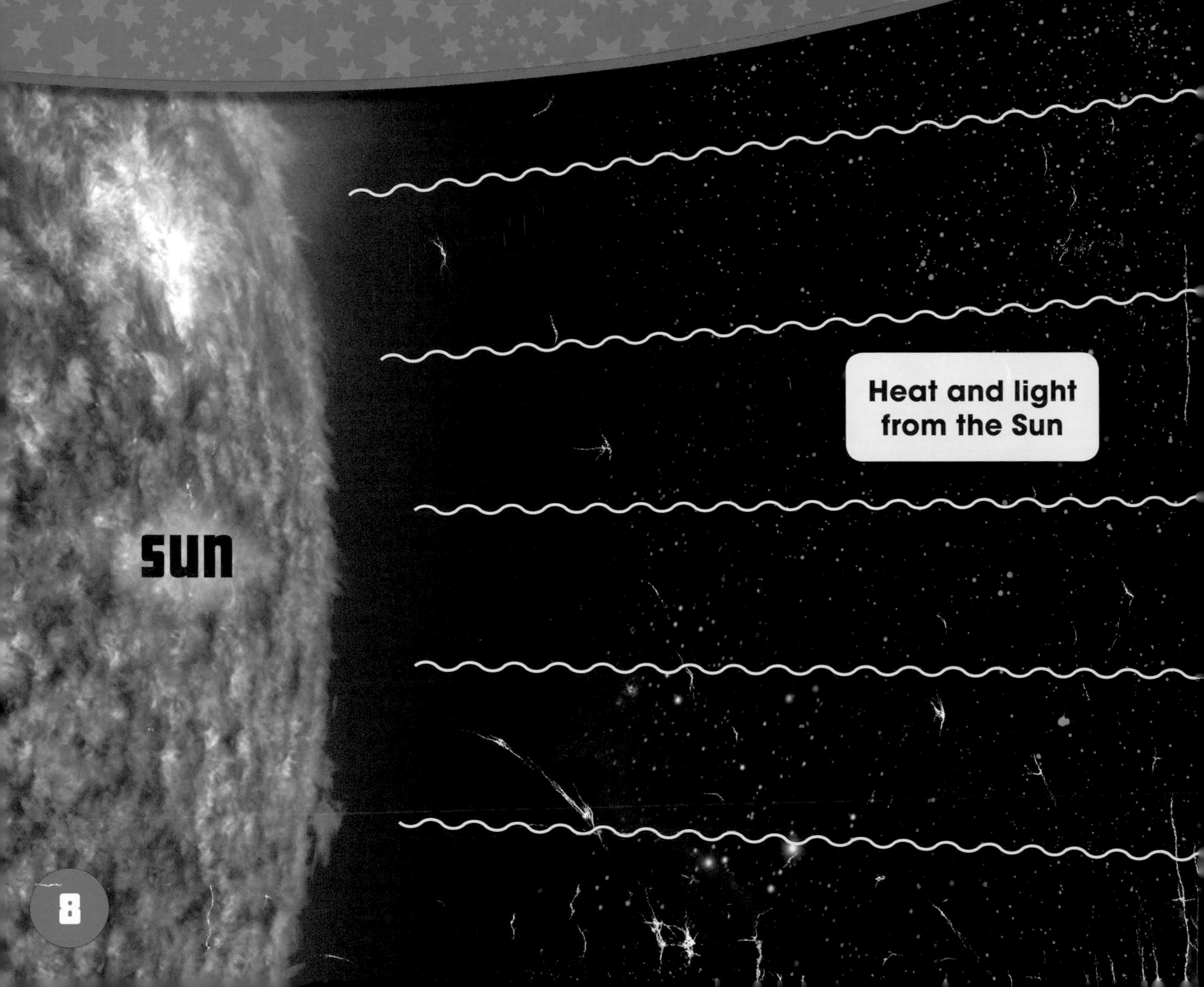

sun

Heat and light
from the Sun

8

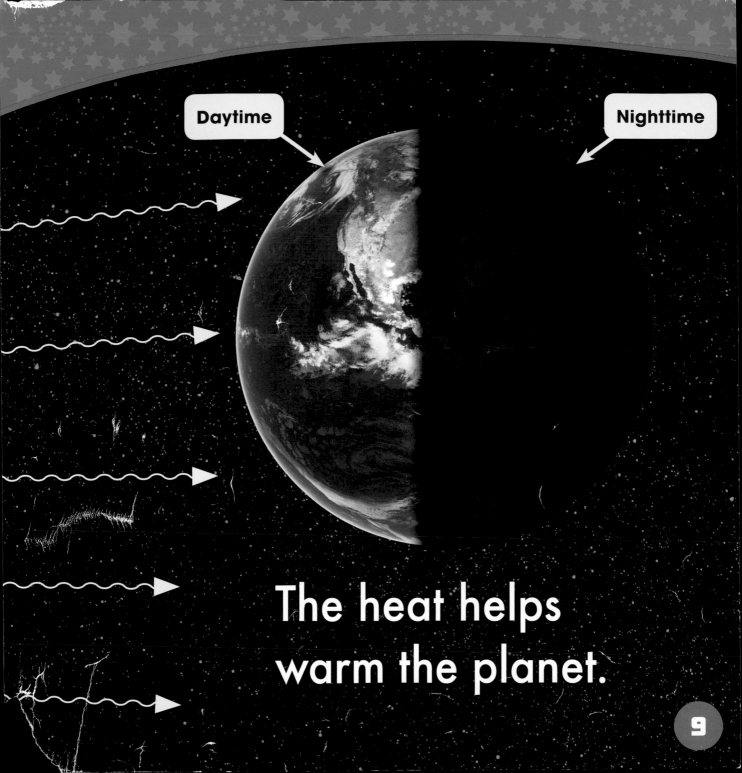

The heat helps warm the planet.

Many kinds of animals and plants live on Earth.

They need the Sun's warmth
and light to live and grow.

Oceans cover most
of Earth.

Ocean water

No other planet in our has liquid water on its surface.

The rest of Earth is covered by land.

Land

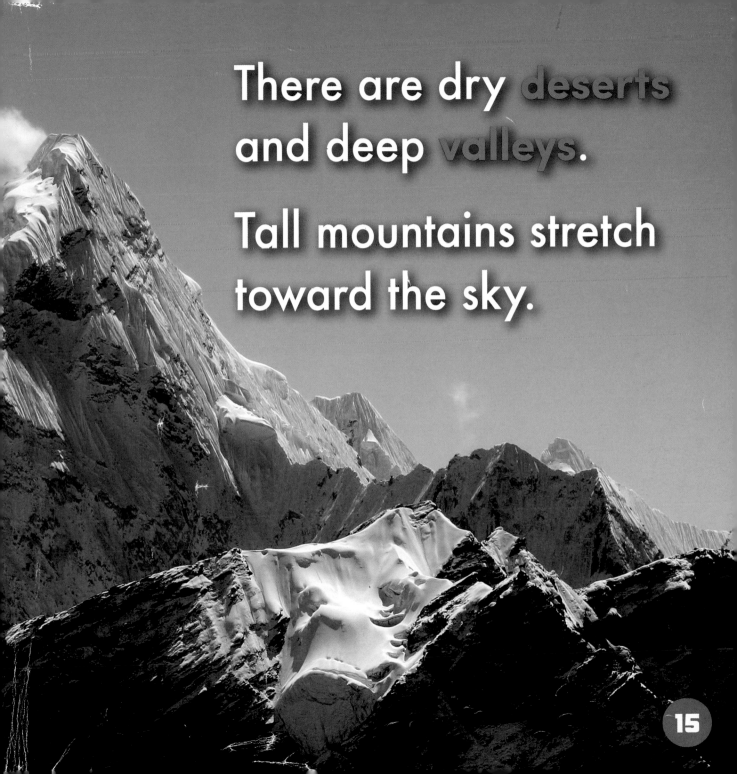

There are dry deserts and deep valleys.

Tall mountains stretch toward the sky.

15

Oxygen and other gases surround Earth.

Animals and people breathe in oxygen to live.

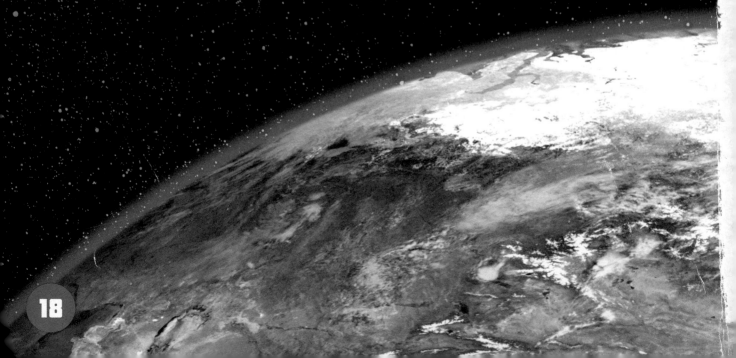

So far, scientists have not found living things on other planets.

To look for them, scientists send spacecraft into space.

A rocket leaving Earth carrying a spacecraft inside

19

One day, we may
discover new life
far, far away!

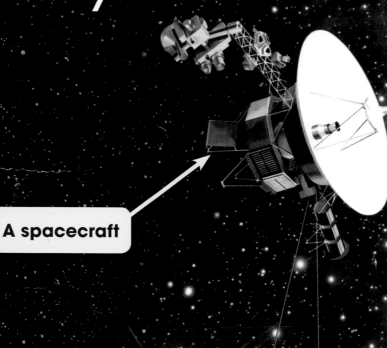

A spacecraft

EXTREME EARTH FACTS

AGE OF EARTH	4.5 billion years old
DISTANCE FROM SUN	92,956,037 miles (149,597,870 km)
HOTTEST TEMPERATURE	134°F (56.7°C)
COLDEST TEMPERATURE	-128.6°F (-89.2°C)
BIGGEST OCEAN	The Pacific Ocean, covering 59 million square miles (153 million sq km)
TALLEST TREE	A California redwood tree named Hyperion at 379 feet (115.5 m) tall
BIGGEST ANIMAL	A blue whale at 100 feet (30 m) long

GLOSSARY

deserts (DEZ-urts) dry areas where little rain falls and few plants grow

gases (GASS-iz) substances that float in the air and are neither liquids nor solids; many gases are invisible

oxygen (OK-suh-juhn) a colorless gas found in the air that humans and animals need to breathe

Solar System (SOH-lur SISS-tuhm) the Sun and everything that circles around it, including the eight planets

spacecraft (SPAYSS-kraft) vehicles that can travel in space

valleys (VAL-eez) areas of low ground between two hills

INDEX

READ MORE

Carney, Elizabeth. *Planets (National Geographic Readers).* Washington, DC: National Geographic (2012).

Lawrence, Ellen. *Earth: Our Home in the Solar System (Zoom Into Space).* New York: Ruby Tuesday Books (2014).

LEARN MORE ONLINE

To learn more about Earth, visit
www.bearportpublishing.com/OutOfThisWorld

ABOUT THE AUTHOR

Joyce Markovics has written more than 30 books for young readers. She lives along the Hudson River in Tarrytown, New York.